A FORTH and CLYDE CANALB

by

GUTHRIE HUTTON

Tram crossing Bainsford Bridge, Falkirk

© Copyright 1991 Guthrie Hutton
First published in the United Kingdom, 1991
By Richard Stenlake, 1 Overdale Street, Glasgow G42 9PZ
Tel: 041-632-2304

ISBN 1-872074-10-3

Barrack boats and soldiers of First World War period. Who they are and what they are doing on the canal is not known!

In the Second World War stop locks were built at Maryhill, Firhill, and Port Dundas which could be closed to prevent flooding had the canal embankments been bombed.

INTRODUCTION

The idea of a Forth and Clyde Canal had been around from the time of Charles II, but after the Bridgewater Canal was built near Manchester in 1761 a 'canal mania' gripped men of commerce all over the country. Many schemes were proposed for Scotland's ultimate prize. In Glasgow they wanted a barge canal centred on the city, in Edinburgh; a 'Great Canal' from sea to sea, by-passing Glasgow. Eventually, after furious lobbying and debate, a compromise was reached and approved by Parliament.

The plan was to leave the Forth by the Carron River to the first lock at the Grange Burn. The route west was through the valleys of the Bonny and Kelvin Rivers to Stockingfield (Maryhill) about three miles west of Glasgow where a branch would take the canal nearer to the city. The proposed terminus on the Clyde at Dalmuir Burn was later changed to Bowling Bay.

Work began on 10th June 1768. After nine years it had reached Hamilton Hill in Glasgow, but stopped there for lack of money. About eight years later funds from forfeited Jacobite Estates were made available to complete it to the Clyde in 1790. The Glasgow Branch was also extended in 1790 to the new 'village' of Port Dundas — named in honour of Lord Dundas, governor of the Canal Company.

It was 35 miles long, with another 3½ miles of the Glasgow Branch, 60'0" wide, 9'0" deep and rose to 156'0" above sea level through 20 locks on the eastern side and 19 on the west. The 'system' was extended when the Monkland Canal was joined to the Port Dundas basins in 1793 and the Union Canal to the main line at Camelon in 1822.

The Caledonian Railway acquired it in 1867 as a condition of buying the Port of Grangemouth. It remained under railway management until 1948 when it was taken over by the British Transport Commission and passed to the new British Waterways Board in 1962. In the same year, Parliament decided to close it and on 1st January 1963 all rights of navigation ceased.

But it didn't disappear along with the railways and trams, closed at much the same time. So early in the 1970's enthusiasts started a campaign for restoration which gathered momentum through the 1980's. An old Clyde passenger ferry renamed 'Ferry Queen' started to operate in 1982 as a pleasure boat and was quickly joined by others. British Waterways and the Local Authorities began a programme of rebuilding bridges and other general improvements. Restoration started on the remaining canalside buildings and where there were none to restore, new ones were built. And are still being built, or restored, or developed; the story of the Forth and Clyde Canal isn't finished yet.

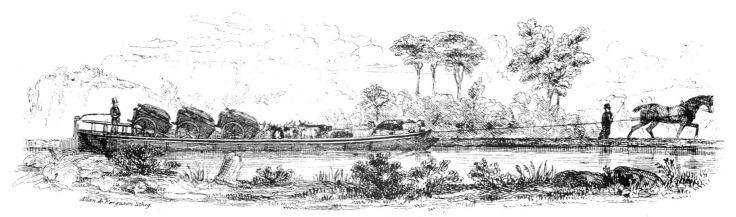

CANAL CART BOAT.

CANAL RAILWAY WAGGON BOAT.

The canal was the wonder of its age and inspired others. The world's first practical steamboat, 'Charlotte Dundas' was built as a canal tug in 1802, but was banned, despite successful trials, for fear that the wash from the paddle wheel would damage the canal banks. The 'Vulcan', the first iron boat built in Scotland, fared better. She was launched in 1818 and was still afloat sixty years later. A replica is now at the Summerlee Industrial Museum in Coatbridge.

As well as these famous innovations the Forth and Clyde Canal pioneered the shipping of loaded carts and waggons directly onto boats, pre-dating cross channel ferries by almost a century.

Allan & Ferguson lithog.

CANAL PASSENGER BOAT.

187 Trongate, Glasgow.

Canal Night Passenger & Goods Boat.

There were three developments of early passenger boats. Track boats with goods and passenger accommodation took a day to go between Port Dundas and Lock 16 at Camelon. Passage boats carrying only passengers cut the journey time to under six hours. Finally 'Swifts' reduced it to just three. Passenger boats had priority and the swan neck on the bow of the 'Swift' is a scythe — an incentive to others to drop their tow line. Such was the demand that night boats known as 'Hoolets' (owls) were also introduced. Stage coaches, the only other form of passenger transport, established feeder services to the cleaner, safer and more comfortable boats.

The ban on steam power was lifted in 1828 and a number of tugs with stern paddle wheels appeared on the canal. In 1856 however, experiments with screw-propelled boats led owners to realise that this was the answer to their towing problems and they quickly put engines into their boats. The first purpose built screw-propelled vessel, the 'Glasgow', was built in 1857 at Swan's boatyard at Kelvin Dock, Maryhill. She is regarded as the first puffer.

These early steam lighters at Camelon Bridge show the clear canal barge lines of boats which, despite their origins, became known as 'Clyde puffers'.

6

69960 (JV.)

Early puffers had their exhausts turned up through the funnel to assist draughting. This produced the distinctive sound and the name. The practice was done away with in later boats but the name stuck. There were three different types of puffer. The 'inside boats' or steam lighters were used only on canal or dock work, 'shorehead boats' — like this one entering Lock 35 at Drumchapel — were developed for work in the Clyde estuary and 'outside boats' which could be used on the open sea and became such a familiar feature of the West Coast.

LAUNCH AT KIRKINTILLOCH.

Built at canalside yards at Grangemouth, Falkirk, Kirkintilloch, Port Dundas, Maryhill and Bowling, puffers were launched broadside into the canal like the 'Tuscan' here at J & J Hay's yard at Kirkintilloch Townhead. The trick was not to stand opposite the boat as she entered the water or you could be drenched by the wave she sent across the canal. Schoolchildren in Kirkintilloch would get a half holiday on the day of a launch.

The Hay's puffers had names like 'Briton', 'Gael', 'Trojan', etc. One of their original boats the 'Saxon' was used as the 'Vital Spark' by the BBC in the television adaptation of the Para Handy stories and two others the 'Boer' and the 'Inca' were used for the famous Ealing comedy film the 'Maggie'.

The 'Arab' — not a Hay's puffer despite the name, is seen here leaving Lock 16 at Camelon going east. A puffer as heavily laden as this was described as 'smelling the bottom'. Drawing 8′0″ she would have been at the limit of operating depth.

The 'Swifts' did not disappear completely with the advent of railways and continued to serve small canalside communities. The last swift, a steamer 'Rockvilla Castle', was broken up in 1880 after the tragic drowning of her owner, Mr. George Aitken of Kirkintilloch.

Aitken had used 'Rockvilla Castle' for pleasure cruises as well as scheduled services. This clearly impressed his son James who started his own cruising enterprise in 1893 with a small steamer 'Fairy Queen' which he replaced with a larger boat, 'Fairy Queen 2' in 1897. This picture of the first 'Fairy Queen' at Craigmarloch amply demonstrates her instant popularity and the need for Aitken to replace her with a larger vessel.

Aitken's next steamer 'May Queen' — seen here at Cadder — was built at Kirkintilloch by Peter McGregor and Sons in 1903 and was the favourite steamer of his daughters Jessie and Mae who I met in the late 1960's.

She is believed to have been 75'0″ long, too long for the locks and as she always sailed on the canal summit this could be true. Also, foreshortening could have been built in, because McGregor's specialised in building boats in sections to be reassembled once they had left the canal. The local joke was that they built the longest boats in the world with the bow in Bowling and the stern in Kirkintilloch.

"GIPSY QUEEN" AT HILLHEAD KIRKINTILLOCH.

'Gipsy Queen' was launched in 1905 at Paisley to become the third boat in Aitken's fleet. She was the largest boat to sail on the canal.

There was a piano on board and the musicians were 'paid' by passing round the hat. One man told me how one day he and his wife spent the last of their money on the fare and had nothing left for a cup of tea. He offered to take over from the pianist who readily agreed and went off to collect money, "and do you know", he said "I played that piano all the way from Lambhill to Craigmarloch and back and never saw that pianist again — or the money!"

12

KILSYTH HILLS FROM CRAIGMARLOCH

A6307

The 'Queens' went from Port Dundas to Craigmarloch. In the early years there was nothing there. If it was a nice day people could have a picnic, but if it was wet there was no shelter. So Aitken built a bungalow tea room. A putting green was set out and swings were provided. A scow converted into another tea room and called the 'Meadow Queen' shared the adjacent basin with two well fed swans known as 'Jock' and 'Jean'.

This picture from the late 1930's shows the much extended bungalow, the remains of the old 'Meadow Queen' and a lone family at the swings. 'Gipsy Queen' was scrapped in the spring of 1940.

GRANGEMOUTH FROM THE AIR

A 65010 JℛV.

The eastern Sea Lock was at the mouth of the Grange Burn and the wee town that grew up around it was called Grangemouth. The canal runs diagonally from the centre left side of this aerial view to the bottom right hand corner. In the foreground is the Carron River with the shipbuilding yards. Above the canal are the extensive timber basins where logs were left in the water to prevent them drying out and cracking as they seasoned. Timber was a principal commodity carried on the canal and today Grangemouth remains a centre of the timber trade in Scotland as do areas of Glasgow beside the canal.

14

The big barges on the Forth and Clyde Canal were called lighters. The smaller boats that could also navigate the Monkland Canal were called scows. Lighters were towed by two or more horses, scows by one. Scow is an old Scots word meaning flat bottomed boat.

An empty lighter is seen here alongside in the basin between the Sea Lock and Lock 2. These unglamorous craft were rarely the subject of photographs and usually appear only incidentally in pictures of something else.

A hand written note on the back of this postcard describes this as 'New bridge at No.2 lock, Canal Street, Grangemouth. 1951' This was one of three such bridges in Grangemouth, so timber and other commodities could be taken direct from the docks into the basins through two other entrances. The docks were closed to commercial traffic during the First World War, hastening the commercial demise of the canal. Trade, mainly in pig iron and timber coming through the docks into the canal, never recovered.

16

CANAL STREET, GRANGEMOUTH. 36854. J.V.

The front steps from the houses in Canal Street led straight onto the cobbled canalside, across the canal were the timber basins. Not surprisingly therefore the message on the back of this card reads "Accidental 'dooks' are quite common here as there is water on almost every side". Sadly, canal and street have both been destroyed.

Partly obscured behind the lock gates in the foreground is a log raft. Often logs would not be loaded onto boats, but simply rafted together and towed along.

The boat coming through the original Bainsford Bridge is one of the Carron Company's large fleet of steam lighters. They were mainly used to convey pig iron from Grangemouth docks to canalside foundries. Crews on this trade from Grangemouth to Glasgow had to complete punishing round the clock schedules of loading, unloading, bunkering and travelling with only a few hours sleep snatched in a hammock.

BAINSFORD SWING BRIDGE. 377.

FB SERIES.

Bainsford and Camelon Bridges were rebuilt in 1905 as swing bridges for Falkirk's new tram service. However the Caledonian Railway (the owners of the canal) would not allow the bridges to be used because uprights supporting the overhead cable obstructed the towpath. The trams had to stop either side of the bridges until March 1906 when the gantries were rebuilt with an extended cantilever over the towpath.

This picture of Bainsford Bridge shows the original gantry as built in 1905.

1269

An extended flight of locks takes the canal up from Bainsford to Lock 16 at Camelon. This is Lock 9 with a scow being worked through it going west. Just below the lock is a swing bridge carrying the railway line into Falkirk Grahamston Station. The Canal Company's Tophill depot, carpenter's shop and boat building yard, was between this lock and Lock 10. Many of its early boats were built here and it was adapted to build iron boats in the 1820's. Experiments in steam power were also carried out here, ironically because Charlotte Dundas, the world's first practical steamboat, had been abandoned at the yard.

THE UNION CANAL AT LOCK 16, CAMELON

A. 8146

This is not the Union Canal as the card states, but the Forth and Clyde looking down to Camelon Bridge. Lock 16 is the best known lock on the canal because the little bridge on the extreme right is where the Union joined the Forth and Clyde through a large basin called Port Downie. The Union Inn, built beside the basin, catered for 'Swift' passengers. Chemicals were the main industries at Camelon and Port Downie. A spectacular fire destroyed the tar distillery on Guy Fawkes night 1973; molten tar poured from ruptured tanks into the canal, causing major pollution which has only recently been cleaned up.

Industrial Bonnybridge. (Eclipse over all)   Published by Wm. Welsh, Springfield Studio, Bonnybridge

arrived safely last night. will write fully very soon. 8/1/07.

This picture from 1906 shows the impressive extent of the iron founding and associated industries that dominated Bonnybridge. In the less prosperous 1930's, the Smith and Wellstood Foundry and Columbian Stove Works operated a job sharing scheme where brothers or father and son would work half a week each. The scheme paid off, because when things picked up the foundry had an experienced workforce ready to go full time. More recently a mural depicting the inside of the foundry was painted on the outside wall.

22

This interesting if indistinct picture shows steam lighters at the Bonnybridge bascule bridge. Bascule is a French word meaning see-saw which aptly describes the operation of these attractive little bridges. Boat crews had to assist bridge and lock keepers — the puffers managed this without stopping by means of one of the crew hanging onto the derrick which was swung out to drop him on the towpath. Other boats kept a bicycle on board — one of the crew got fit cycling between bridges and locks.

As motor transport took over from horses the little bascule bridges were replaced by steel swing and lifting bridges that could cope better with the increased volume and weight. Here at Castlecary the swing bridge also became a bottleneck on the main road between Glasgow and Stirling so when the road was upgraded to dual carriageway in the early 1960's, parliament closed the canal instead of spending £160,000 to replace the bridge. It was a suspiciously convenient reason to close a canal that had become politically unpopular. The consequences are still with us.

BANKIER DISTILLERY.

It wasn't the water in the canal that attracted distilleries but the plentiful supplies of grain and fuel that could be reliably obtained by being beside it. The main canalside distilleries were Port Dundas — said to be the largest in the world, Rosebank at Camelon Bridge and the one shown in this picture Bankier near Denny, built in 1828 and only recently demolished. The canal loading point and elevated roadway connecting it to the distillery can be clearly seen. Like many distilleries, Bankier also kept (presumably happy) pigs, fattened on the waste draff.

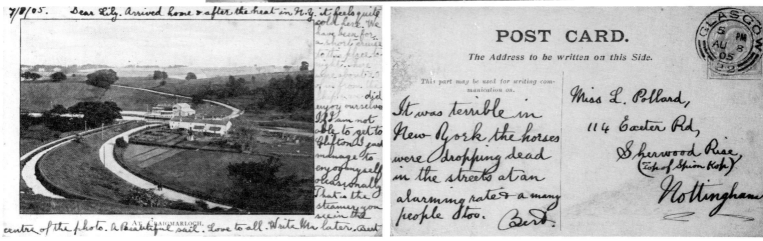

At CRAIGMARLOCH.

7/8/05. Dear Lily. Arrived home & after the heat in N.Y. it feels quite cold here. We have been for a short cruise to the place to-night, where we are about 4 of us from the ship. We did enjoy ourselves. If I am not able to get to Clifton's I can manage to enjoy myself occasionally. That is the steamer you see in the centre of the photo. A beautiful sail. Love to all. Write Mr later. Bert.

POST CARD.

The Address to be written on this Side.

This part may be used for writing communication on.

It was terrible in New York the horses were dropping dead in the streets at an alarming rate & a many people too. Bert.

Miss L. Pollard,
114 Exeter Rd,
Sherwood Rise,
(Top of Spion Kop),
Nottingham

Water ensured the canal's survival after closure. The top picture shows Townhead Reservoir (also known as Banton Loch), a canal reservoir created on the site of the 1645 Battle of Kilsyth. Parliament gave the canal owners the right to divert water into reservoirs within ten miles of the canal, so long as they didn't deprive existing users, like mills. Lades feed the water down to the canal, sluices and run offs control the level. Even with the canal closed, millions of gallons flow through it every day making it an essential feature of present day land drainage. The lower picture with the interesting account of a New York heatwave, shows the feeder lade from Townhead Reservoir curving round beside the road to meet the canal at Craigmarloch.

Craigmarloch looking east to the Dullatur Bog — an innocuous scene now, but — John Smeaton the canal engineer thought he could drive the canal through the bog filling it with water at the same time ... but it didn't quite work out that way. The cut kept filling up with slime and defied efforts to clear it. Over 55′0″ of earth and stones were sunk to build up the banks and towpath and a stable disappeared into the bog. The bodies of men and horses that had fled from the Battle of Kilsyth and perished in the bog were uncovered. And after all these problems had been overcome, millions of frogs, looking for a new home, spread like a plague over the countryside.

Mineral deposits were a major factor in determining the line of the canal and revenue from their extraction was a feature of costings for the various routes proposed for the canal. Quarrying was the main industry of Auchinstarry, just south of Kilsyth.

The disused flooded quarry on the north side of the canal has now been landscaped to provide parkland and picnic areas beside a lagoon and climbers use the huge rock faces as practice walls. A new boat, Gipsy Princess, uses the canal for pleasure cruises.

There is evidence of small and large scale quarrying all over the area between Auchinstarry and Twechar, but the main industry of Twechar was coal — neatly avoided on both sides in this picture of 'Fairy Queen 2'. The colliery on the north side of the canal was provided with a railway swing bridge on condition that they maintained shipments of coal through the canal. They continued to do so long after others had switched to railway transport.

Local miners and quarrymen going out on a Friday night would tell their families that they were "... awa to gie the bully ma money". The 'Bully' was (and still is) the Quarry Inn.

Road and stream share the same cobbled base under the canal through Shirva Pend, this little aqueduct just to the west of Twechar. People were luckier than horses because they could walk on the raised path seen on the right of the picture. Another similar aqueduct at Bonnybridge employs the same cunning device of combining road and stream and must have saved the canal builders the considerable cost of duplication.

Kirkintilloch harbour at Hillhead became Scotland's first inland port when trading began between there and Grangemouth in 1773. Most goods to and from Glasgow started or completed their journey on carts.

On holidays, so many boats were tied up in the harbour that people can still remember walking across them from one side of the canal to the other. At one time drink flowed so freely in Kirkintilloch that the town became famed for its drunkenness. After a deed poll banned it in the 1920's, Kirkintilloch became famed for being dry. Certainly pubs show up prominently on old postcards — of the canal!

The great single arch span of the aqueduct over the Luggie Water at Kirkintilloch began the important section of canal west to Glasgow. Despite being beautiful in its simplicity the aqueduct became famous as 'The Unique Bridge' when the Campsie Branch Railway used it as a route to cross the canal. The Luggie was culverted under the two smaller arches in front of the aqueduct, with the railway on top. The card was published by Aitken's Emporium, Kirkintilloch — so 'May Queen's' presence in the picture would doubtless be mandatory!

Townhead Bridge, Kirkintilloch.

This busy scene at Townhead Bridge, is also from Aitken's Emporium. Kirkintilloch is the nearest thing to a canal town in Scotland and its industry is the whole canal in microcosm. Iron founding, boatbuilding and repair, nickel smelting, timber and coal. Ironically it also became one of Scotland's first railway towns in 1826 when the Monkland and Kirkintilloch Railway was built to bring coal to the canal basin.

Kirkintilloch had to be isolated during an outbreak of cholera in 1832. Horses were stopped a mile either side of the town, their barges towed through by the (suddenly very popular) stern paddle wheel boats.

The canal almost overlaps the Antonine Wall, and many Roman artefacts were unearthed when the canal was being cut. The 'wall' was a huge earth bank fronted by a ditch and topped by a turf and timber pallisade. Behind it forts and fortlets were spaced out across the country. Today, planning constraints might force a different route, but the canal drove through the wall and its associated structures in a number of places. At Cadder it runs along the ditch for a short distance before taking this 90° bend through the wall (the high tree-topped mound on the right of the picture) and the remains of the fort were quarried for stone to line the banks.

34

Cadder is the prettiest and (if you believe all the memories of former 'Queen's' passengers) the most romantic spot on the canal. The cottages with their gardens running down to the water's edge, the kirk nestling in the trees, the old mill (which pre-dates the canal) on the left of the picture and the woods with distant views of the hills all combine to create a magical setting. But Cadder has its dark side too. After the Union Canal was opened, bodysnatchers from Edinburgh raided the Kirkyard. Perhaps they got the idea from the infamous Burke and Hare who both worked as labourers on the Union Canal.

The change from town to country is very sudden at Lambhill on the northern edge of Glasgow. The large building on the left of the picture is a stables — known to canal men as 'horse barracks'. These were built to a standard pattern at set stages along the canal and were used to provide fresh horses for the Swifts. Iron, steel and coal were the local industries.

Lambhill witnessed one of the most emotional funeral scenes in Glasgow in August 1913 following the fire disaster in which 22 miners died at the nearby Carron Company's No.15 Cadder Pit.

36

"Gipsy Queen" at Firhill Bridge, Glasgow

The outside of a 90° bend at Firhill was widened to form one timber basin, another, shaped like a kidney was formed on the inside. The tow path was in effect an island — much appreciated by wildlife today. Glass making, attracted to the canal by the combination of sand quarrying and coal was one of the main industries of Firhill, and Murano Street in the background of this picture is thought to have been named after Murano Island near Venice, famed for glass making. The Firhill iron works is still there. So too is Glasgow's other football team, Partick Thistle.

Glasgow's Highest Chimney, Townsend.

Glasgow became effectively a port on the east coast as well as the west when the canal arrived and can trace much of its industrial ascendancy to that time. In 1790 the Clyde was shallow and tidal so when the canal was completed ships preferred to come up to the city by canal. Port Dundas quickly became a very busy place and busier still when the Monkland link was completed in 1793. And according to the early handbill improvements were still being made in 1842.

The most conspicuous landmark on the 'Cut of Junction' between Port Dundas and the Monkland Canal was Tennant's Stalk, a chimney over 450′0″ tall at Tennant's Chemical Works. It was demolished in 1922.

Picture postcards were issued in huge numbers in the early years of this century, but apart from the 'Queens' and places where the canal was central to a town not many were produced of a canal that was then unfashionable. This is certainly true of Port Dundas which in a Glasgow context must have been very low on publisher's priorities.

This photograph of Ann Street Bridge was taken by the daughter of the bridge keeper. One childhood memory often recalled is the excitement of a walk up Ann Street to join 'Gipsy Queen' at her berth beside the bridge.

Like Port Dundas, there are few old postcards of Maryhill so I am indebted to my friend Drew Sommerville for this picture of midget submarine 'XE 1X' passing Kelvin Dock in 1952. Many people remember the mini-sub's voyage — but few remember the date.

Maryhill is quite magnificent. There are five locks Nos. 21-25 joined by irregular oval basins. At the foot of the locks is the Kelvin Aqueduct and between Locks 22 and 23 is the Kelvin Dock (where the first puffer was built). The dry dock has an ingenious conduit system for draining it into a lower basin and the whole complex is linked as a continuous work of masonry. Beside the Top Lock is the White House pub, a canalside original.

40

John Smeaton retired as engineer when construction started again in 1785 and was replaced by Robert Whitworth. He designed the Kelvin Aqueduct, the largest then built in Britain. It has four arches supported by buttressed piers with arched spandrels — clearly visible in this postcard — It is 400′0″ long, 70′0″ high and was built between 1787 and 1790 at a cost of £8,500 — it should have cost £6,200.

The area behind the aqueduct is known as the Butney. This is believed to be a corruption of Botany Bay and it is thought that either convicts were shipped from here or the aqueduct employed convict labour or maybe working on it just seemed like penal servitude! No one really knows.

A magic-lantern slide from 1894 of a mean looking dog standing in front of Lock 27 at Temple. The bascule bridge spanning the lock chamber was replaced by a massive lifting bridge in 1932 when Bearsden Road was realigned. There is an impressive working model of the new bridge in the Royal Museum of Scotland in Edinburgh. On the right of the picture are stacks of timber, presumably belonging to Robinson Dunn's timber yard which was cut in half by the new road, but continued to operate, until recently, on either side of both road and canal. A new pub 'Lock 27' has been built on the site of the old lock keepers cottage and it has a fine display of old canal pictures on the walls.

42

This is the third of four locks in the Boghouse flight and like Temple the bridge has been placed on the lock sides instead of being built separately. The Drumchapel and Knightswood housing schemes had not of course been built when this picture was taken and the locks were then set in pleasant countryside. Each lock had a fall of about 8'0" and could accommodate boats 68'6" long and 19'8" wide.

Kilbowie Road and Canal Bridge, Clydebank

Kilbowie Road and Dumbarton Road Bridges were both replaced with drowned culverts when the canal was closed and the water shallowed by partial infilling between Linnvale and Dalmuir. All this makes future restoration difficult, but not impossible! Another Clydebank canal was more completely filled in by the Caledonian Railway; the Forth and Clyde Canal ran half a mile from Whitecrook to the Cart opposite the mouth of the River Cart. It was opened in 1840 as a link for Paisley into the Forth and Clyde but it was not a success and was closed in 1893.

Singers moved their sewing machine works from Bridgeton in Glasgow to a new factory at Kilbowie in 1885 to become the biggest industrial concern on the canal — and in the world! A railway station was named after it and the huge clock was the biggest in Britain.

At its peak in 1913 the factory produced over 1,300,000 sewing machines with a workforce of 14,000. At that time much of the production went to Russia, but after the Revolution other European markets had to be developed. Most of the factory survived the Clydebank Blitz, including the clock but fortunes declined after the War and in 1980 it was closed and demolished.

Yes they made ships and sewing machines, but ask anyone from Clydebank or Dalmuir about the canal and they will talk about goldfish. The theory is that someone emptied a tank of fish into the canal. The fish survived and — as in the best fishing stories — grew to prodigious sizes, in water warmed by the outflow from Singers works. Fishing for coarse fish was and still is, one of the most popular activities on the canal.

Fishing boats would sell fish fresh from the sea to canalside customers. Today, customers at canalside supermarkets in Clydebank can buy fish in a plastic bubble with a 'sell by' date — and they call it progress!

46

Canal Bridge, Dalmuir

82531. ⓙⓝ

Trams used to stop either side of Dalmuir Bridge until it was replaced by this swing bridge in 1915. The lessons of spanning the towpath with a cantilevered gantry seem to have been learned from Falkirk.

The No.9 Auchenshuggle to Dalmuir West was the last tram to run in Glasgow — and it ran over Dalmuir Bridge. The message on the back of this card tells its own story — "I am having a nice holiday, went on one of these cars yesterday to Glasgow. It was a long ride. I shall have such a lot to tell you when I come back". — Ever thought of Dalmuir for your next weekend break?

Ferry Road, Old Kilpatrick.

'Ferry Road' was the road to the Erskine Ferry. The bascule bridge was replaced by a swing bridge in 1934. Beside the Canal House is a signal box belonging to the Caledonian Railway who squeezed a mineral yard between the canal and the Clyde.

With the river so close, the canal doesn't seem to have brought any substantial industry to Old Kilpatrick. The Shell Mex oil barge 'Mexdee' operated from a berth adjacent to the Admiralty Oil Storage Depot east of the bridge.

48

THE LOCKS OLD KILPATRICK

The Erskine Bridge has now replaced both bridge and ferry and it towers over Lock 37. The Kilpatrick Hills form a dramatic backdrop to the lock and beckon travellers on the last lap to the Clyde and the sea.

The canal and Antonine Wall were well separated west of Cadder, but true to form as soon as they came into contact again at Ferrydyke just west of Old Kilpatrick the canal cut straight through the bath house of the Roman fort.

THE LOCKS, BOWLING

On 28th July 1790 the commitee of management and the magistrates of Glasgow sailed in a large track boat to Bowling to perform the opening ceremony and pour a hogshead of water taken from the Forth into the Clyde to symbolise the union of the eastern and western seas. In August the 80 ton fisheries sloop 'Agnes' sailed from Leith to Greenock to complete the first crossing from sea to sea.

When the canal was closed the locks and basins were maintained as a rump of working canal to provide the only fresh water moorings for boats on the Clyde.

The Swing Bridge, Bowling.

The fishing boat is actually going through two bridges, a bascule and the huge elevated Caledonian Railway swing bridge. At one time Bowling would boast that from this bridge five public ways could be seen: The Caledonian and North British Railways, the River Clyde, the road from Glasgow to Dumbarton and the Forth and Clyde Canal, and that at no other place in the British Isles could this be seen!

"Just finished my 58 mile tramp to this place by the Union and Forth and Clyde Canals" is the message on the back of this card — Bowling is the end of this pictorial tramp along (just) the Forth and Clyde too.

SELECT BIBLIOGRAPHY

Strathkelvin District Libraries and Museums have published a number of excellent small books:-

Don Martin	The Forth and Clyde Canal — A Kirkintilloch View, 1977.
A I Bowman	Kirkintilloch Shipbuilding, 1983.
A I Bowman	Swifts and Queens, 1984.
Paul Carter (Editor)	Forth and Clyde Canal Guidebook, 1985 & 1991.
A I Bowman	The Gipsy O'Kirky, 1987.

Other Publishers:-

Jean Lindsay	The Canals of Scotland, pub: David and Charles, 1968.
Alan Brotchie	The Tramways of Falkirk. The N.B. Traction Group, 1975.
Dan McDonald	The Clyde Puffer, pub: David and Charles, 1976.
A I Bowman	Symington and the Charlotte Dundas. Falkirk District Council Department of Libraries and Museums, 1981.

ACKNOWLEDGEMENTS

On winter. nights I give talks about the canal and am indebted to the many people who have shared their memories with me at these talks. I am also indebted to my old friend and 'drouthy cronie' Donald McKinnon whose similar talks are an equally rich vein of anecdote.

I must also acknowledge the superb work done to preserve the memory of the canal by Don Martin at Strathkelvin District Libraries and thank him for his assistance with this book. I must also thank Pat Malcolm of Clydebank District Library.

And Ian Bowman, alas no longer with us. Without him the story of the canal would never be told properly. Simply a wonderful man.

DO YOU REMEMBER?

I 'discovered' the canal not long after my return from Australia in 1962 and was appalled that my fellow Scots could be so short sighted as to destroy it. I never lost that feeling and some years later started to preserve what I could, collecting canal related material, mainly old picture postcards. This book is the result.

But not the end of the collecting. Writing this has confirmed for me the importance of gathering these pictures and memories together — and the need to search for more. If you have memories or old photographs somewhere — it doesn't matter how small or apparently insignificant, I would be delighted to hear from you — please contact me through the publisher.

Guthrie Hutton.